A Smidgen of Smatterings

Donna Rooney

BookLeaf Publishing

Presentation by *BookLeaf Publishing*

Web: www.bookleafpub.com

E-mail: info@bookleafpub.com

ISBN: 9789395950589

First edition 2022

I am dedicating this first book of poetry to my loving family. Thank you for always being there for me.

I love you all so much!

ACKNOWLEDGEMENT

I would like to acknowledge my family; my husband, Bruce, (who bought me my first laptop with which to write when we didn't even have the money) and my children; Emily, Nicholas, Eliza, DeAnna, and Marshall for supplying me with endless material with which to work. I'd also like to acknowledge my six grandchildren for, without them, the world (and my poetry) could not go on. Lastly, I'd like to acknowledge my parents-- for without their constant love and support, I would not have become the woman I am today.

PREFACE

This little book of poetry was first conceived using my mother's old typewriter when I was a child. The first poem included here is a testimony to my ten-year-old belief that I could-- one day-- write a book. Life happened, and my poetry got caught up in the whirlwind of emotion and time. I hope you enjoy a cup of your favorite coffee or tea and read the heartfelt poetry in store for you here.

Halloween Night: A child's first poem

The night was black
as a witch's cat.
The stars were fuzzy and dim.
The moon was round
as a plate in the sky.
The children were laughing again!
For it was Halloween night
and quite a sight
to see the children run.
It only happens once a year
But oh! It's so much fun!
To dress up like a monster
and collect the candies and then,
run on home before it's too late
and count up your candies again!

Autumn Diamonds

As I sat inside
I looked outside
And as I did
I saw a big
BUG
on a dandelion.
The autumn leaves
Were changing from green
Yet shone like
Diamonds
under the sunny sky
as the wind whispered by
like baby's breath.

Sun Sparklers

Sunrays like Fourth of July sparklers shoot
across the surface of the salty sea.
Their fire roared at my feet as I stood on the
shore by myself.
Even the gull's white wing reflected the
bejeweled waters.
So thankful for this moment in time
Locked away for safekeeping in the recesses of
my mind
This moment which shan't be taken from me
This moment that was meant to be.
The never-ending lapping of my shimmering
sea.

Spring Time

The laughing wind with its wistful breeze,
Blew gently through the sycamore trees,
And as it did, the sun shone through
Revealing a most alluring blue.

A scarlet bird flew o'er the fence,
And into the forest so very dense.
A small red spot he left behind,
His image forever in my mind.

A flower I noticed so lonesome and small,
Said, "Don't worry sonny, someday I'll be tall."
"But have no fear, there'll be others here,
We'll bloom for a while, then you'll see us next
year."

A beautiful day it was sure to be.
As the warm, friendly, creek invited me.
And as I laid back, I could hear it say,
"What a wonderful, wonderful, wonderful day!"

Unbeknownst to Me– My Future Husband

Sitting beside me, beneath the sun-drenched skies, is a man.
An ordinary man I suppose, in a sense.
His body strong and solid shimmers with perspiration,
as he gazes silently at the multi-colored sails drifting across the glassy lake.
He reaches into his pocket, and I notice how large and well-defined his hand is,
moving with such tangible grace.
Shifting his weight to better observe the artistic display before us,
I see the light cast from the water dancing in his eyes.
His cinnamon-colored eyes seem to hold a magical depth–
so placid and tranquil that one often wonders where this calmness comes from.
He is a good man and possesses a sincere and unselfish character about him.
His heart, capable of engulfing the universe, is presented through his kind and loyal way of life–
an inherent gift, I fancy.

As his eyes meet mine, I feel a sense of warmth envelop me
Shattering all thoughts and inhibitions.
His boyish charm is transmitted through his gentle smile,
And then I realize– this man I love.
9/20/85

Looking Back on Twenty Years…

Shadows growing longer in the throes of imminent maturity,
The rearview mirror now holds the answers to questions of our youthful spring.
Many stopping places we have visited along the path,
Now beaten down from the weight of familiarity.
Markers, tallies, and feathers have been accumulated in the quest.
We have grown wise to some, ignorant to others,
Yet we continue to walk together,
propelled by curiosity to see how long the shadows will stretch.
We observe the natural beauty of a sunset that we knew would follow
And realize that after the rain, after the winter's cold, and after the scorching heat,
that amidst all in which we have endured– that this is who we are:
Comfortable and worn friends.
A quiet understanding is shared- silent communication absorbed between souls.

Sails on lakes forgotten over time, lie faded in the folds of memory.
Yet some snapshots remain, touched by time and acquired knowledge.
Cinnamon-colored eyes still hold that magical depth,
but now also hold a new dimension- a wisdom unforeseen.
The sky now holds the hues of old Valentine's tucked away.
Shadows growing longer in the throes of imminent maturity,
And yet I realize– this man I will always love.

March 8, 2006 (Our 20th anniversary)

The Haiku Lake

Old man winter sleeps
Banks of budding crocuses
Purple haze abounds

A chorus of frogs
Much anticipated song
Spring peepers arrive

Pink buds overhead
Trees swaying in harmony
Sights and sounds of spring!

Red

No other color in the spectrum we see
Has more emotion than red, to me.
It's the color of extremes from love to hate,
there really is no debate–

Of red's power.

Red is passionately aggressive with vitality!
Yet dangerously dominant and holds the key.
Red is blazing sunsets over pastures and lakes
And also of sweet smelling Valentine cakes,
That symbolizes love with devotion and hope
For without love we could never cope–

Without red's power.

A crackling fire on a cold winters night
Red's warmth holds us captive, tucked in very
tight.
It's excitement and confidence on the 4th of July
When family and patriotism are at an all-time
high!
We feel it as we watch the sky–
The exploding power of red in cascades.

Red draws attention when caution is needed
High alert! Be careful! This must be heeded!
But being festive red's a twinkling tree,
With gifts wrapped in paper for you and me.
Is there any color more versatile than this?
I'll leave this for you– a red-lipsticked kiss!

God's Country

The eastern sun just above the horizon kissed the
cedar-filled mist line
where orange-mango melds with the pink
overtones of sheer beauty.
How lucky am I to be the only one standing here
in this small spot of time?
Fencelines draped with the cascading symphony
of fat-headed grasses heavy with dew,
as small purple petals push their way through
exclaiming, "Me too! Me too!"
The breathtaking beauty–only a snapshot of
time,
Becomes the cornerstone of this rhyme.

Home Sweet Home

How wonderful to get away
From responsibilities.
To romp and play just like a child
Leave work behind, and rest awhile!
It sounds so tempting, please let's go NOW!
A plane? A train? I don't care how.
We'll need a sitter for the pets
I guess we can drop them off at the vet's.
I know it's expensive to leave them there,
But that's okay; we'll make it up somewhere!
And don't forget we'll need to pack
It'll be a long time before we get back.
I'll need half the cabinet for makeup you see,
And then I'll pack even MORE things for me.
I'll need a large assortment of clothes,
With this weather, no one ever really knows!
And then there's what type of shoes I should wear,
I had better bring several or buy even more there!
I may need new luggage, I don't think it all fits,
This packing has brought me to the end of my wits!
I don't know if this is really worth it to me,
I'm working this hard just to be "free?"

For Pete's sake, we really could just stay home–
We'll tell them we've gone and just be alone
to sit and enjoy this life that we have
and not worry about packing and all of those
bags!
You know this IS a nice place to be–
And best of all, it's practically free!
What do you think? Are you feeling less
stressed?
I think, in the end, our home is the best!

Limerick

There once was a turtle named Red
With stripes on both sides of his head
“I’m free!” so he thought,
‘Till a child caught him up,
Now he waits in a tank to get fed.

For the Love of a Reformed Maniac

Is there anything more lovely than a soft and furry friend?
One that loves you unconditionally until the very end?

But in between the waiting for your work to be "all done,"
Your bestie might get bored with that and decide to just go RUN!

RUN up the wall to the windowsill to see outside and then
tear out down the hallway and then race back in again!

By now you're thinking, "How crazy; whatever's got into him?"
But about that time he's scaled the fridge and is dangling from the rim!

He seems to have gone completely mad! "Who is this imposter?" you ask.
"Where is the old fellow that naps in a chair in the sun's rays, while he basks?"

About that time the wild-eyed thing begins to
look around
You're not quite sure what's coming next then
he's off again with a bound!

This time his newest interest lies in a plant that's
by the door
You run to stop the damage but he plows
through it like a boar!

By now you're quite exhausted as you've just
cleaned up the mess
"A little bit of quiet time sounds best, I must
confess."

You fluff your favorite blanket when a familiar
friend arrives.
with purrs and snuggles quietly taking the
blanket on your side.

"Oh! There you are" you say to the reformed
maniac
"So glad you're here– your evil twin must've
decided to go back!"

Is there anything more lovely than a soft and furry friend?
One that loves you unconditionally until the very end?
Zzzzzzz Zzzzzzzz Zzzzzzzzzz

For My Loves: A Medley of Salutes

Emily

You've always been our little girl;
And in our hearts, you'll be
The same sweet gift- a little pearl
In an ocean of uncertainty.
Always do what's right in your heart
And search for the good in others.
We are so very proud of you,
With love, your Dad and Mother.

Nick

A crossroad in the highway of life also called
"Graduation"
is a reason to celebrate-
and reflect
on past accomplishments,
as well as failures to learn from and avoid.
On this lifelong venture, it's a good idea to
slow down,
look both ways,
proceed with caution,
and anticipate others' moves
to be prepared for the unexpected.
Stop at all rest stops and scenic views so you can
stay in touch
with what really matters.
Sometimes it's not how fast you arrived at your
destination,
but the manner in which you proceeded.
Wiggling those ears is a great way to proceed!
Congratulations!
Love, Mom and Dad

Eliza

Remember the tree that you proudly gave me for
"Earth day"
all those many years ago?
Like you, it has also grown to be beautiful, tall,
and sturdy.
I have watched it grow outside my window,
as I have watched you grow outside the window
of my heart.
It too has survived tough, angry storms
As well as beautiful sunny days.
Yet it blossoms every spring
and reminds me of my precious baby girl
born under the same birthstone color
18 years ago.
My sincerest hope for you, Eliza,
Is that you will continue in your strong ideals
and faith
as you branch out into various fields of interest
in your life.
We wish you the best of luck today and always,
and remember,
we are always so very proud of your
accomplishments!
Love always,
Mom and Dad

DeAnna

You hold a special place in our hearts,
the youngest daughter and all.
You're spirited, bright, and loving,
yet you too will "fly" in the fall.
A void will be felt forever
when you leave us for new sights,
But confident we are in your teaching-
You're ready to take that flight.
We've molded and taught you the best we knew how.
Now it's up to you to take that last bow
and embark on the journey of what lies beyond.
Just remember young starling the strength of our bond.
May good health, love, and happiness follow
you wherever you roam.
Love Always,
Mom and Dad.

Marshall

The youngest of five, we knew you'd arrive
at this day sooner than the rest.
It's been your lifelong goal to grab and take hold
of whatever freedoms you could possess.
And so we held you a bit closer perhaps-
Selfishly knowing you were the last chance
We had– to see magic thru a child's eyes.
But this day arrived as we knew it must
to take you too, on the uplifting gust
Of lands unseen, dreams unchecked, of wishes,
wants, and desires.
Keep it true to yourself, and the man upstairs,
Take on the challenges- but not all the dares,
You've got this "Hims," of this we're sure.
There ain't no way you'll be deferred
Don't look back and don't be sad,
We love you so much- from Mom and Dad.

Diamante Poem Cat/Dog

Cat
Soft, sleepy
Purring, kneading, meowing
Whiskers, claws, collar, tags
Barking, digging, licking
Frolicky, frisky
Dog.

Field of Daisies

Every Memorial day we were forced to ride
around the Midwest in a station wagon for
hours.
It was a big deal to them–
But we didn't really understand the
significance–
Mother saved coffee cans throughout the year
for this very day.
Now the cans were "decorated" with aluminum
foil
Mother thought they looked nice.
We took stakes to hold the cans upright;
My father made them out of old coat hangers.
The peonies–hundreds of them– filled the back
of the car with their pungent aroma.
Mother cut them early and kept the buds in the
refrigerator for this special day–
The perfumed memory stays with me still,
etched into my mind.
We traveled from one cemetery to another,
placing fresh arrangements on graves
of people my brother and I had never met.
Tissues, red noses, and stories told at each stop.
At one cemetery there was a field of wild daisies
beckoning me to come closer.

Feeling sorry for those people who had no flowers at all,
I began picking a few wild daisies for them.
How sad I thought in my young girl's mind,
To be completely forgotten over time.
When the adults were done with their chores,
They looked back at all the graves dotted with a single daisy laid upon the headstones–
More tissues, red noses, and hugs for me.

“Home” is Where You Are

Thank you for this glorious day
The wind, the trees, the hint of rain.
The cacophony of endless sounds
From big to small, your creation abounds!

When worries seem to burden me,
I look up into the old ash tree,
And see how carefree the little birds sing
because, Dear God, You are EVERYTHING!

You walk with me when I am blue
And on those days when I can’t make it through
And even in the dark of night
I feel, Dear God, your strength and might.

I know that I am not alone
Living in this world called “home”
But we all know it’s borrowed time
Until with you, we’ll truly shine!

But in the interim, I thank you so
For the blessed beauty, you have bestowed
And patiently wait for what heaven brings
When we’ll go “home” and you’ll be out King.

A Mother's Learning Curve

Upon bringing a child into the world,
one's filled with emotions-
Fear, and love,
gratitude, and endless joy
...but the fear is real.
Can I do this?

I've never been at this job before.
I need to teach her so much more!

This world's not the same as when I was small
I feel like I'm new here- I know nothing at all!
But I trudged on,
Trusting the Lord knew what was best-
"How can I be given this task, Lord?
She crawls in bed with me when it storms."
I soothe her fears-
tell her "It's just the angels bowling;
we have nothing to be scared of"
Or do we?
She's back to sleep
drifting on reassuring words
while I listen-wide awake- to the wicked storm
outside
Rumbling...winds blowing....

When kindergarten loomed near,
I was certain she couldn't possibly be ready–
Only five years?

I've never been given this job before-
I need to teach her so much more!

But that big, yellow bus came,
And swooped her away…
I cried all that day.
I found after that week
that she was more ready for school–
than I
when she exclaimed that the "baddest boy"
in her whole school
had the most beautiful handwriting.
"He can make all the letters perfect!"
She had been watching him
From her five-year-old window…
"Everyone has something good about them,
Mama."
I didn't worry so much after that...

Although I had never had this job before,
She's going to teach ME –a whole lot more.

What Kindness Means To Me

If I were an earthworm on a rainy, flooded path,
Kindness would be a helping hand to lift me
back to grass.

If I were a ladybug struggling in the pool.
Kindness would be a saving net-- a very helpful
tool!

If I were a kitten or a little playful pup,
Kindness would be a ball of yarn or fresh water
in my cup.

If I were a horse or cow on a cold and windy
day,
Kindness would be a loving pat and a great big
bale of hay.

But even though I am none of those, I still could
use a hand,
to help me with so many things I don't quite
understand.

So if I ask a question would you please be nice to me?
I have so many questions about who I want to be!

For all God's creatures big and small, what should kindness mean to you?
To me, it's being nice to all-- even when you don't want to.

Kindness is the "Golden Rule" that all of us should know.
Treat others how you'd want to be and peace and love will grow!

The Showdown

The initial leader's a beauty to see,
Dressed in his most shimmering green.
His adversary is also a gem to behold
for in his suit is a glittering gold.

The fight goes way back between these two
gents.
It's always the same- as they continue to vent.
They size each other up they rise and they fall,
their eyes on the prize- Oh! The drama of it all!

Just when it appears a victor is had,
another young fellow steps in with a jab!
A petite pretty lady keeps her eyes on the duel
from a safe distance- she isn't a fool.

And then they're all gone in the blink of an eye
I shake my head and turn with a sigh.
I may never know if a winner was found,
I'm just a spectator of this hummingbird round.

Saved by the Storm

Our sweet farm dog, who had just turned four,
Was acting quite odd as she sat by the door.
She looked almost sad with her tailed tucked under
I went outside thinking, "It must be the thunder."

I looked here and there, and to and fro,
I found her ball and gave it a throw.
She happily brought it back to me
I decided the 'ole girl just wanted to play, you see.

But a little bit later, it happened again.
She was sitting out back by the doghouse pen.
This time she was pacing with her head down low,
Then she flopped down as the wind began to blow.

I said to my husband, "Dear, there's something wrong;
Your dog's been acting strange all the day long."
His eyebrows knitted in a frown as he left
And he came back in later with something under his vest.

“What do you have?” I inquired with worry,
But the kitten he revealed was nothing but furry.
“Is that what’s been bothering the dog all the day?”
I guess Ruby’s a hero and her new friend will stay!

Words

And in the end, it's all just words–

Words of congratulation, "Way to go; he's
almost an 11-pound boy!"
Words of encouragement, "You can do it!"

And there are the hushed, quiet, words of sheer
exhaustion and joy,
"Look Mom; look what I did" when I met my
first grandchild.

All words echoing in the hallways of my mind–

Some good memories,
"I want you's neck, Mama" spoken by a
sleepy-eyed son.

Some bring back pain when I remember,
"There's been a change in your father's
condition"--
Left as an impersonal message when my father
had passed.
–I never got to say the words "Goodbye" or "I
love you" just one more time.

Words.

There are words of jealousy, “That’s mine!”
heard so often that
I’ve lost count.

Some words come with a bit of a cringe, like
“Can we keep him?” Egads!!

My mother told me countless times before she
died,
“I just love dimes!” Why? I don’t know, but
The words are in my head whenever I see one.

There are special words to issue support and
comfort–
words of faith and hope for the future.

There are words of peace like “Peace be with
you.”
That we don’t use as often as we should.

And of course, there are too many words used
for hatred.

I prefer the words of love and appreciation–
As I’m sure most would.
This follows the “Golden Rule” of doing to
others

As you would have them do unto you.
What a great way to live– if only all of us would follow it.

Words.

Why do we all have access to language,
But so few of us use it correctly?

Words should bolster and help at all times,
Not tear each other down.

Whether words rhyme or not,
Please always know that I love you a lot.

www.ingramcontent.com/pod-product-compliance
Lightning Source LLC
Chambersburg PA
CBHW051743130826
49812CB00033B/984
9789395950589